Life Poetry

Denise M. McCollin

authorHOUSE®

AuthorHouse™
1663 Liberty Drive, Suite 200
Bloomington, IN 47403
www.authorhouse.com
Phone: 1-800-839-8640

© 2008 Denise M. McCollin. All rights reserved.

No part of this book may be reproduced, stored in a retrieval system, or transmitted by any means without the written permission of the author.

First published by AuthorHouse 5/7/2008

ISBN: 978-1-4343-7933-7 (sc)

Printed in the United States of America
Bloomington, Indiana

This book is printed on acid-free paper.

Dedicated to all women

You are all pillars of strength and even though at times you may not understand why a situation is happening, just have faith that the experience is a lesson needed to get you to a better, more enlightened state.

Contents

Introduction: My Life	2
Acknowledgments	5
Nothing Lasts Forever	7
I Long to See Your Face	9
I Am Thankful For You	11
Thank You	13
This Feeling	15
I Love You Too	17
Me	19
I Want	21
Your Presence	23
Tired	25
Let It Go	27
Do You Know?	29
The End	31
What I believe	32
Only Two Things	35
God, What About Me?	37
Love Is the Only Reason	39
Second Time Around	40
Still In the Game	43
Here and Now	45
One and the Same	47
Slow Down	49
Change	50
Finally Here	53
Eternal Love	55
You	57
Guide Me	59

Introduction: My Life

Being denied for who I was because
    I had red hair and freckles
Having Pa walk me to the school ran by Ms. Beckles
Spending a lot of time at my aunt Elaine,
    though I'm not quite sure why
She'd always send me to the store owned by
    Mr. Johnson to trust instead of buy
Eating Eclipse biscuits and being forced
    to drink powered milk
Not wanting to call my father's mother gran,
    but doing so to avoid guilt
She made really good suck-a bubby treats
    and the greatest macaroni pie
I will never forget my asthma attacks; many
    times I thought I would die
My father's house in North Friendship Drive…
    why can't I say it was our house?
Because what I remembered there was abuse
    and mom tip-toeing like a mouse
The next door neighbors, Shelly and
    Linda, with them I'd play
Their mom and dad seemed happy and at their
    house I wished I could have stayed
Moving back to my grandma, ma's house
It was very small, no inside toilet;
    I had to use the scary out house
My grandmother taught me much about spirituality
    and drawing strength from above
From walking me to school, to washing my
    hair, everything was done with such love

Watching my mother struggle working hard
    to give my sister and me only the best
The prettiest Sunday school dresses, Christmas
    feast, she never settled for less
Moving from Barbados to America, so homesick
    at times I didn't want to get out of bed
Being on my own at seventeen, one night
    not knowing where I'd lay my head
My first real job as a CNA, my first apartment,
    it wasn't easy being all alone
It was frightening at times but I was determined
    to succeed, I was now grown
Climbing the ladder to become an RN,
    while supporting me was no easy task
No time to play, I worked hard, studied
    hard and busted my ass
Buying my home, my short marriage, miscarriages,
    divorce, deception, hurt, pain
I asked why, not realizing that through it all,
    knowledge and blessings were gained
Relationships that lasted for a while, what
    I thought was a waste of my time
When I look back, a lot was learned, I now know
    that they were allowed by the Divine
Gaining religion, loosing religion, in the process
    becoming more spiritually in tune
My life, I've realized, is to infect everyone with
    the love I have inside…no one is immune.

Acknowledgments

For everything and everyone in my life, I thank God, the Divine source of all things. My purpose was laid out long before I came on the scene of this life and for this I say, thank you God. I especially thank my mother Elma L. Watson and my father Arthur P. McCollin because without them I wouldn't be here to experience the great process of this life. My sister Cheryl V. Mc Collin has been a steady source of encouragement. I thank you sis for your listening ear and for critiquing my work. To all the lovely nurses that I work with, thank you all for taking the time to read my work and giving me your feed back. Sorry I made a few of you cry with the words I wrote, but it showed me that what I write will have an impact on those who read it. To Donald E. Thompson Jr, thank you for inspiring, for encouraging, for loving and for believing in me. To everyone who has entered my life, I say thank you all for the lessons you've taught me. Some were painful, some were joyful but they were all needed.

Nothing Lasts Forever

Don't wait until tomorrow
See it, hold it, and savor it now
Cause nothing lasts forever
Love it, caress it and cherish it now
Cause nothing lasts forever
Don't hoard it, lord over it or abuse it
Cause nothing lasts forever
Spend it, share it and give it away now
Cause nothing lasts forever
Believe it, receive it, and achieve it now
Cause nothing lasts forever
Enjoy all of life's goodness now
Cause nothing lasts forever

I Long to See Your Face

Baby, I long to see your face
The thought of this causes my heart to quicken its pace
I long to look into your chestnut brown eyes
Because something deep inside, tells me that you are my prize

I want to experience the reality of my dream come true
From our many conversations, I'm convinced that this is you
It may seem that things are progressing with much haste
But honey, I long to see your face

I want to touch the man that is you
Having your presence in my life seems way past due
But then again, I have to believe that nothing happens out of place
And now darling, I long to see your face

I can't wait to feel your lips against mine
To be held in your arms until the end of time
May this be the beginning of a love that we both embrace
Because baby, I long to see your face

I Am Thankful For You

I thanked God today for you
For allowing our paths to cross
I believe that my desires were heard
But in actuality the Divine already knew
Knew the desires of my heart
To meet a man just like you
A man filled with love, integrity and values
You are a gift that no other source could have impart
Impart something so wonderfully pure and true
You are my ideal man, very loving and oh so fine
May my heart be forever filled with gratitude
Because I thank God for allowing me
    to meet the man that is you

Thank You

Thank you for showing up in my life
And being that beam of sunlight when
    my skies seemed a bit gray
Thank you for reminding me that there
    are still good black men out there
Men who are good fathers, productive, loving
    honest and faithful to their women
Each and every day
Thank you for possessing such a unique
    communication style
Where we can talk about anything
    from A-Z with ease
Having fun all the while
Thank you for openly discussing your past,
    your future, your hopes and dreams
Thank you for including me when you
    speak of things yet to come
I really like what that means
Thank you for respecting me and my opinions
    even when they differ from yours
Thank you for being so gentle,
    so romantic and so passionate
Every time without fail you know how,
    where and what it takes
To relieve my ache
Thank you for that amazing way
    you look into my eyes
Every time you do, I blush and feel like
    I'm the most beautiful woman alive
Most important of all
Thank you for being the special man in my life.

This Feeling

What do I call it, this feeling that I feel
I feel a comfort level that is so surreal
It feels like I've known you for a lifetime at least
When I'm daydreaming about you, I'm filled with such peace

What do I call it, this feeling that I feel
After a conversation with you, my heart and soul feels healed
I've told you my secrets, my hopes and my fears
From the way that you listen, I know you are one who truly cares

What do I call it, this feeling that I feel
The moment I first saw you, I was filled with passion and zeal
Couldn't wait to kiss you and hold you close
Being in your presence is what I enjoyed most

What do I call it, this feeling that I feel
Respect, security, admiration, could this all be real?
I feel happiness and contentment
    that can only come from above
I know what I'll call this feeling… I'll call it love

I Love You Too

You say that you love me
And baby, I love you too
There's nothing in this world that
    I wouldn't do for you
This is not infatuation, nor is it lust
I have this amazing feeling deep inside
    when I think about us
The physical is great, but that's not all it's about
I'm in love with your entire being,
    the feeling is devout
I knew there was something special about you
    the day I heard your voice
And after meeting you, it was confirmed,
    I had made the right choice
You are so warm, so affectionate,
    so loving, and so kind
There is no doubt that you were sent to me
    from the Divine
You tell me that you love me
And baby, I know that this is true
Not just from your words, but from
    the things that you do
I care about you deeply
You are my dream come true
And yes baby, I love you too.

Me

Can you see me for me?
Remove the blinders of what you think I should be
Look at the kind, intelligent, graceful
    woman before your eyes
Recognize that you have indeed found a prize

Can you respect me for me?
Different background, spiritual belief
    and unique personality
There is no need to always agree
Appreciate the differences that may always be

Can you accept me for me?
A genuine soul, being all that you see
A generous person willing to give all
You only have to ask or simply just call

Can you love me for me?
Leaving out the judgment and hypocrisy
Whether you can or not, there is still
    much love within my heart
A gift to you, I so freely impart

I Want

I want not to be one of many passing in the night
I want you to not only lust after my body
I want you to make love to my soul
I want to be the only one that you behold

I want to never doubt anything that you say
I want to call you mine and have you call me yours
I want to love you, support you and
    always be on your side
I want to believe your words and be able
    to walk next to you with pride

I want to see my unborn child when
    I look into your eyes
I want to always be close to your
    warm and loving embrace
I want to know that you'll forever be
    by my side and always have my back
I want it to be us against the world,
    shielding each other, no matter the attack

I want to view you as not just a typical man
I want you to be my king, the one I can submit to
I want to be your queen, the true love of your life
I want to look at you and be able to envision
    the day; I'll become your wife

Your Presence

When I'm in your presence
I can't keep my eyes and hands off of you
There is a bond between us
We both know it, this is nothing new
You put me at ease
With the way you hug and kiss on me
I love to see you smile and laugh
It brings me joy to see you happy, relaxed and free

When I'm not in your presence
I can't help but think the worse
I know too much about your player ways
Women are your curse
I've heard you say you love me
So many times before
Why should I believe it this time?
After you've been through so many women's doors
I want to, I wish I could
But I don't trust a word that you say
There is a big price for loving you
With my heart, I'm no longer willing to pay

Tired

I'm tired of fussing and cussing
Tired of acting like less than the Queen that I am
Tired of settling for less than I deserve
Tired of plotting ways to make you hurt,
    like you've made me hurt
Tired of waiting for karma to give you yours
When is this going to stop?
I'm tired, God knows I'm tired
Tired of being hurt, mad and sad
Even though you don't hit me physically
I'm tired of being your punching bag
Tired of this mental exhaustion
Tired of this emotional tension
Tired of hearing you say I'm sorry
Tired of forgiving and giving chance after chance
I'm so tired, God knows I'm tired
Lord, I'm tired of being tired

Let It Go

The guilt, the pain, the shame, let it go
The heartache, the abuse, the misuse
The lies, the misconception, the deception
Being taken advantage of, fear, feeling like no one is there
Not being treated fairly, loss, paying inflated cost
Dreams that didn't come true,
    that guy who wasn't right for you
Not giving it your all, being lazy, acting crazy
Impatience, intolerance, hate, not being able to relate
Disappointment, greed, lust, creating unnecessary fuss
Investments that didn't pan out, causing
    you to scream and shout
Mud on the floor, spilt milk,
    loosing your temper way too quick
Anger, calling God's name in vain and acting truly insane
Feeling unworthy now and then, because
    you don't fit that size ten
Friends who always lack, smile in your
    face then stab your back
The relationship that brings anxiety
    instead of joy and security
Dwelling on things that aren't note worthy
Don't let it stop your flow, drop it all and let it go.

Do You Know?

Do you know what it feels like?
To love someone who doesn't love you
Its gut wrenching, it's torture
My heart is more than broken in two

Do you know what it feels like?
To have someone toy with your emotions
Making me feel unworthy of true love
When I know that I deserve a better portion

Do you know what it feels like?
To give chance and chance again
Only to end up right where I was before
I feel alone in this world without a friend

Do you know what it feels like?
To be betrayed too many times to count
Not even morphine can dull this pain
All I can do is scream and shout

Do you know what it feels like?
To finally say, "Enough is enough, I'm done."
It's liberating, such a sweet release
I'll stay strong and believe that the best is yet to come

The End

My heart is breaking
My soul is aching
Was it love that we were making?
Or were you just faking
I thought you were my dream come true
I was so excited to have met you
Things started out really fast
But I was convinced that this would last
As they say…all good things must come to an end
I just can't wait for my broken heart to mend

What I believe

I believe that our paths cross for a reason
And though some relationships last but for a season
There is always a lesson to be learned
Greater knowledge of self, others and life is earned

I didn't come into this world today
I admit that from past experiences,
    some things do cause me fear
I've been cheated on, lied to, deceived and more
So now I believed that as you get to know
    someone, trust will grow

I am happy and proud of the woman I've become
But I'm wise enough to believe that
    the work is not yet done
My heart is so filled and over pouring
    with unconditional love
And I give thanks alone to God above

I believe in myself and what I have to give
With love, joy, kindness and understanding
    is how I want to live
We may not always see eye to eye
But believe me, when I say that I love you,
    I will till the day I die

I am not looking for the most handsome or richest man
But I am looking for someone who will
    accept me for who I am
Knowing full well, that we both are a work in progress
The goal is to remain steadfast and
    committed through all of the stress

A relationship is two working together
    for the betterment of both
Where you are weak, I'll be strong and so forth
I am in this for the long run
And I believe that with love and understanding,
    there's nothing we can't overcome

Only Two Things

There are only two things that I want in this life
One is to be a mother and the other, to be someone's wife
It seems that these two things are eluding me
God, when will these two things be bestowed by thee?

There are kids having kids everyday
Not wanting the children and throwing them away
Where is the justice, where is the sense in this?
When I hear of such situations, I can't help but to be pissed

Children are being tortured, abandoned, neglected and abused
Even one instance is too much, but the activity is profuse
God tell me why these things are allowed?
When my dream of becoming a mother
    seems as far off as a cloud

God, where is my husband, the man made just for me?
How long before I meet him, how long will it be?
I'm trying to hold on, but my body is getting weak
My heart is hurting; my soul is crying and
    my spirit becoming bleak

There are only two things that I want in this life
One is to be a mother and the other, to be someone's wife
It is time that these two things stop eluding me
God, I'm asking that these two things be bestowed by thee

                    •

God, What About Me?

My God, my God, where are thee?
I am right here, do you see me?
I've been asking, pleading and begging you
I'm at my wits end, what else am I to do?
Am I not deserving of being someone's wife?
Don't you think I'm worthy of that type of life?
I've been praying and waiting and waiting and praying
My God, please, what are you saying?
Where is the man that the universe created just for me?
When will I meet him and be able to shout with glee?
I'm tired of boys who pretend to be men
God, where is the one who will be my lover and friend?
Sometimes I think that you don't care
At times I wonder if you even hear
Just in case you haven't, I'll say it again
Heavenly father, I am growing weary, I can't stand the pain
I'm thankful for my life experiences that
    have caused me to grow
I'm truly grateful, even though at times it doesn't show
Every relationship allowed has taught me something new
About others and about changing some things that I do
In my heart, I believe that my prayer will be answered soon
So help me shake off this feeling of gloom
I'll have faith that you have heard me
I'll have faith that there is a man created just for me
I'll have faith that soon he'll be right here with me
I'll have faith that it is already done for me
So I say Amen and so shall it be.

Love Is the Only Reason

When I look into your eyes, I see a piece of me
We're all connected eternally
I see your struggles, your pain and your joy
I'll always be here for you, I won't ever be annoyed
You can call on me morning, noon or night
I'll lend a helping hand, whatever your plight
If I ever see you down, I'll offer to lift you up
Know that we are each a page from the same great book
And on a deeper level, we're all one and the same
Forget about your money, car, house or fame
Contentment, joy and peace is the real goal
Stop, reflect and look deep within your soul
When you're finished reflecting, it will
    all be brought to the light
You'll see that the petty stuff isn't worth the fight
Our physical bodies are on loan to us for a short season
We're here to love God and each other, that's the only reason

Second Time Around

Here we go again, a second time around
At one point I was sure that we had
    run this into the ground
If its love that's drawing us back together,
    why didn't it help us to stay?
I sure don't have all the answers;
    I just know that we both still care

Here we go again, a second time around
Are all of the things corrected that caused
    us heartaches and frowns?
It will take some time to heal and
    get back into the groove
Forgiveness, fidelity and understanding
    is what we now must prove

Here we go again, a second time around
I'm older and wiser, no time for childish
    games and acting like a clown
I've grown and learned much about myself
    and life while we were apart
I've tried to shake you, I wanted to hate you
    but I couldn't get you out of my heart

Here we go again, a second time around
All I ask is that you be faithful and
    honest and not string me along
I promise to love and support you,
    this is the easy task
But I have to work on trusting you and
    letting go of things from our past

Here we go again, a second time around
I believe in us, our love for each other
    is still amazingly strong
You'll be my rock and I'll be your pillar and
    together we can see anything through
This is the beginning of great things to come;
    I believe it this time, I really do

Still In the Game

I'm still in the game despite all of the pain
I've been knocked down, injured and bruised
But I'll still carry on; I'm going to see this through
The final score will be a better me and a better you

I'm still in the game, pushing through the sweat and the tears
I've had some personal and technical fouls
I'll continue to run on this court called us
Our winning basket is coming so let's slow down and not rush

I'm still in the game, ready to work as a team
Blocking and tackling life's trials as they come
I'm trusting that only good things you'll throw
    so I'll be here to receive
Our touchdown will be a great life together,
    this I truly believe

I'm still in the game, even though we've struck out before
Let's stay in this, despite the issues we've bat at in the past
Time to keep our eyes on the ball called love;
    the game is not yet done
Look up, watch our love soar, we've finally hit our homerun

Here and Now

Forget the coulda, woulda, shoulda
Focus on right here and now
Yes things could have worked out differently
But does anyone really know how
Don't focus on the past, accept this new season
You are where you're suppose to be
Cause everything happens for a reason
Change from this moment on and great things you will see
Regret and despair, if you allow can swallow you up
Accept what is and acknowledge your mistake
Proceed to a better tomorrow from here and now
Dwelling on the past only brings heartache
Have faith that greater things are yet to come
Stop wasting time and energy looking back
Just enjoy the moment right here and now
And believe me, there's nothing you'll ever lack

One and the Same

I see me when I look at you
It's wonderful, it's scary but it's very true
I see you when I look at me
You ask; how in the world could this possibly be?
We all originate from the same intelligent, everlasting source
So a piece of God, the Divine, is within each of us of-course
We're players with different faces, all in the same game
Believe it or not, we're all one and the same
Traveling on this journey we call life
Our purpose here is to love not make strife
But we let the devil, the enemy, the Ego get in the way
Then from love, peace and joy we so easily stray
We all do it; it's not unique to me or to you
How can we change this, what can we do?
We must seek aid from the all knowing source within
It's liberating, it's easy and it doesn't cost a thing
Anger, hurt and fear takes us over at times
This is when we need to go deep within to find
The answers, the solution, no need for pain
This source is available to all of us because
    we're all one and the same

Slow Down

Wait a minute, catch your breath and slow down
Who are you running from, where are you running to
Why hurry, what's the rush
Just stop for a while and place your feet on the ground
Pause, relax and stop moving with such quickness
Check you internal speedometer; don't go over your limit
If you do, life may pull you over and give you a ticket
It's called an ulcer, a heart attack, a stroke or just sickness
It's OK to say, no I won't be able to
Don't overly worry about what other may say
Take time to smell a rose or savor a cup of tea
In order to nurture others, you first have to take care of you
Sit down, close your eyes and turn off all sound
Focus only on your breath, clear your mind and let go
Don't be afraid of the silence, embrace this space
For this is where peace arises from,
    when you just… slow down

Change

A change is coming, great things are in store
Pay attention, things won't be as they were before
Follow the new path even though
    nothing looks the same
Welcome, appreciate and willingly accept the change

Go in a new direction, step out of your comfort zone
At first it may seem difficult because
    things are new and unknown
If you keep doing things the same old way,
    the same old results will come
Start walking, talking and moving
    to the beat of a different drum

Readjust the way you react to the small things first
Did the things someone do, caused
    you to fuss, fume and curse
Respond instead by being understanding,
    gentle and kind
A change in that person's behavior is
    what you soon will find

You can change the world, one person at a time
But you have to start with yourself, while
    seeking help from the Divine
When you forgive instead of judge, love
    instead of reacting in fear
All of the obstacles, pain and heartache
    will no longer be there

When you take inventory of your life, it may
    seem that you don't have enough
But when you shift your perception to
    gratitude, you'll see the surplus
You may have a hard time accepting that
    change must first come from within
Great things are in store, the change
    within you is where it all begins

Finally Here

My love, I'm so elated that you are finally here
I will love, respect, honor and cherish you every day
I've waited what seems like an eternity,
    to see and touch your face
Here is where I want to stay, with your hand
    in mine and our fingers interlaced

You are everything that I've dreamed of and so much more
Finally, I completely opened my heart and
    allowed you to walk through my door
To a place of tenderness, warmth, truth
    and unconditional love
Without a doubt, I know that you were
    sent to me from above

I can't keep my eyes off of you; you're perfect,
    so tall, so handsome and so fine
I'm beside myself and overflowing with joy
    at knowing that you are all mine
You're loving, gentle, respectful, funny, romantic and strong
No one who knows you would challenge
    this or say that I was wrong

I always knew, I wasn't created to walk through this life alone
You're finally here and together we'll build a
    loving, happy and peaceful home
To our children, we'll be a shining example
    of how true love should really be
This is the beginning of our life long harmonious
    journey together, just you and me

Eternal Love

I love you more and more with each passing day
It hasn't all been easy
But this is where I'm going to stay
You make me laugh
You've made me cry
You make me moan in ecstasy
Beside you is the only place my soul wants to be
We compliment and complete each other
This love and passion I feel for you
I've never felt for another
I love to hear your sexy voice
It makes my heart leap and sing
I look deep into your brown eyes
And I can see what our future will bring
You are the one that the universe has created just for me
Together in love, is where we'll stay
For all eternity

You

You make me laugh
You make me cry
You make me happy
You make me feel like I could die
You make me excited when I see your face
You make me sad when you leave my place
You make me want to hold and squeeze you tight
You make me so mad at times, I want to fight
You make me see how similar we are
You make me realize that you're the one I want by far
You make me acknowledge my true feelings hopes and fears
You make me see that you are one who truly cares
You make me see how forgiving and loving I can really be
Thank you for making me a better me

Guide Me

Guide me Holy Spirit, on my journey back home
Help me to realize that you are always present
    and I am never alone
When the ego tries to take over, as it often wants to do
May I remember that you are near and
    I can always count on you

Help me change my perspective and see things another way
Guide me Holy Spirit each and every day
When the urge arises to show anything less than love
Remind me that I am greater than my fears
    and I can rise above

No need to get angry, to fuss or to fret
This only leads to saying things that I surely will regret
Guide me Holy Spirit to a place of peace and rest
When I heed your precious voice, I give only my best

Guide me Holy Spirit; you know all of my needs
Help me to monitor and control my
    thoughts, words and deeds
Thank you Holy Spirit for guiding me through this life
When I listen, my journey is smooth
    without conflict or strife.